JOURNEY THROUGH THE VALLEY

Kathy Bernard

JOURNEY THROUGH THE VALLEY

True Events That Inspired
The Favorite

Kathy Bernard

Mobile, Alabama

ISBN 978-1-58169-674-5
For Worldwide Distribution
Printed in the U.S.A.

Evergreen Press
P.O. Box 191540 • Mobile, AL 36619
800-367-8203

To those who have walked

through dark valleys

and been triumphant

Contents

PREFACE

We are all on life's journey, each starting and finishing at different times. The journey has many adventures, opportunities, and mountaintop experiences as well as valleys. What is a valley? It is a low point or another definition is: "Any place, period or situation that is filled with fear, gloom, foreboding or the like, such as the valley of despair" or the valley of death (as mentioned in the Bible). Those valleys might look like sickness, death, divorce, financial troubles, homelessness, loss of job, or rebellious children. The valleys, or low points, in our lives can knock the wind out of our sails, and our lives can feel like they have come to a standstill or even a downward spiral. But there is *hope* in the midst of those valleys. God is still present.

This book is my blog composed during a deep personal valley when my son Luke was in a near fatal car accident. When my family started this journey, I was encouraged to blog our experience to keep everyone informed on a daily basis of Luke's progress. We were at the hospital for twelve to eighteen hours a day. We had a lot of time to reflect, read God's Word, pray, and even sing songs as we were by Luke's side. My blog became more than a status report. It was a special time where God ministered to us through the encouragement of individuals, scriptures, songs, and poems that are reflected in my writings. I believe that blogging our experience was therapeutic for me in walking through our valley.

In the past several years, some have asked to read my blog during a valley in their life. Others have encouraged me to put it in a book form. My family's story is shared to encourage others going through a personal valley. The format is basically what I wrote during that time. I have added some titles, scriptures, and ended each blog with a prayer for *you* and a place to write your thoughts of your personal journey. The particular number of the day in each section reflects when each blog was written and thus shows how quickly we walked through this dark valley (90 days). I blogged the most, and Daniel (my husband) and other family members shared a few times when they wanted to express their thoughts.

So we begin our story with Daniel's thoughts. It will give you a dad's perspective on what he dealt with and experienced during our journey. I pray that as you read this journal of our journey, it will bring hope, encouragement, comfort, and belief that God is ever present and walks alongside you through the low times, and even carries you when you cannot go on in your own strength.

Walk with me through my journey. —Kathy

Acknowledgments

Thanks to Peggy Morris and Jane Stanley who read the blog and gave me suggestions of how to put it in book form.

Thanks to Bethany Reyes, my daughter, who wrote her thoughts in the blog at a difficult time.

Thanks to my husband, Daniel, who shared his heart several times in the blog. He encourages me to be a better person every day and challenges me to do big things, such as write this book.

Let us therefore come boldly
to the throne of grace
that we may obtain mercy
and find grace to help
in time of need.
–Hebrews 4:16 (NKJV)

PROLOGUE

A FATHER'S JOURNEY FOR HIS SON'S FULL RESTORATION

From the end of the earth, I will cry to you; when my heart is overwhelmed; lead me to the rock that is higher than I. –Psalm 61:2

I was on my way to the Houston airport to fly home when I got the call. The manager of the restaurant where Luke worked called us on Monday, March 11 about one o'clock to ask if we had heard from Luke. He had missed work without calling, which is very unlike Luke. I knew immediately something was wrong. Kathy, our daughter Bethany, and I went on a search by internet and phone to try to find out where Luke was. Kathy called hospitals, police department, etc. while Bethany searched the internet and Facebook, communicating with Luke's friends.

At the plane's boarding gate, Bethany called and told me the devastating news that they had finally found Luke, and he had been in a single car accident. He was in ICU at Los Angles County USC Medical Center. The doctors didn't give him much hope for survival with a broken back, neck, and severe brain trauma.

The Southwest attendant, Pierre, changed my flight to LA, charged me $300, and put me in business class. I had trouble keeping my emotions in check and cried during much of the flight to Los Angeles. I arrived at the hospital at about 1:20 on Tuesday morning. Luke was swollen, with his head and his body twice its normal size. He was not moving.

After four hours of praying and reading the scripture over him, Luke finally began moving his arms and legs. I knew then that there was no paralysis and began to praise God! God is faithful! We were heartbroken to realize that for three days Luke had been in intensive care without anyone knowing. But thankfully he was brought to what many people are saying is the best trauma unit on the west coast. His surgeon removed a portion of his skull to extract two blood clots on the outside of the brain so we were also thankful there was no intrusive surgery on the brain.

As soon as I heard the news regarding Luke, I began to quote John 10:10 where Jesus said,

> *The thief comes only to steal and kill and destroy; I* [the life giver] *have come that they may have life, and have it to the full.*

I believe Luke is to be a "bearer of light" in dark places like Los Angeles, and he has not fully moved into his calling. He went to church and participated in Bible study, but had other issues that have affected him. Even though Luke has not been completely honest about his lifestyle, we questioned his wisdom of being out so late the night of the accident. We are asking our merciful God to show His mercy and His power. I know God is merciful but I want to know His mercies in this situation. I immediately rejected any thought that Luke was going to die. Satan may have stolen, but he will not kill Luke. Of course, he cannot destroy Luke because he knows our Savior and Lord. Satan would love to cut off Luke's life before his purpose is fulfilled. No one can tell me that when God created Luke Benjamin that his destiny was to die at the age of twenty-five. No way.

God has created us for good works, which He decided in advance (see Eph. 2:8-10). Luke's purpose and mission has not even begun. Satan cannot kill Luke until his purpose is fulfilled. I cannot pray any other prayer. God is sovereign. He can do anything He wants, but I believe this is not His will. I know that even if Luke was not in God's perfect will that night, God in His mercy, could weave this situation back into His perfect pattern for Luke's life.

• • • • •

Lord, my heart is hurting so deeply and I cry out to you. I cannot bear this pain that I am going through right now. My heart is overwhelmed. I need you God! Help me! Amen.

Reflections

_____

_____

_____

_____

_____

_____

_____

_____

_____

1

THE BEGINNING OF THE STORM

When I am afraid, I put my trust in you. —Psalm 56:3

It all began with a phone call no parent wants to hear—"Your son is missing." Thus began hours of phone calls to find out what had happened to Luke. Nervousness, stabbing pains in my heart, and a stomach twisted in knots describe my feelings during those uncertain hours. All kinds of thoughts tumble through your mind: "Is he dead on the side of the road?" "Kidnapped?" "Arrested and in jail?" "Accident?" "Where is he?"

Once we knew what had happened to Luke, we then had to wrap our minds around it—the injuries and Luke being by himself for three days before we found out. We praise God for Luke's employer who was concerned enough to call us and tell us he hadn't gone to work. It is surreal to think of *our* child being hurt critically and feeling helpless miles away. Daniel was in Texas on business, so he re-routed to head to LA. (It was God's provision that just as he was ready to board the flight for home, we finally got word where Luke was and he switched his flight). I booked the first flight at 5 a.m. in the morning. Both of us wanted to get there as fast as possible to hold our son's hand, pray over him, and let him know he was loved and not alone.

• • • • •

*God, my mind cannot comprehend what has happened,
but I trust you. Help me, God! Give me strength! Amen.*

Reflections

_____

_____

_____

_____

_____

_____

_____

_____

_____

HELP ME PRAISE GOD
FOR THE LITTLE SIGNS (DAY 2)

Come to me, all you that labor and are burdened, and I will give you rest. –Matthew 11:28

We are praising God for good reports today. Luke is breathing on his own...not shallow breaths but deep breathing. He still has a tube in his mouth to continue cleaning out his passageway. X-rays of his brain came back, and they appear normal. Praise God! We will know more when he wakes up.

The surgery was to remove two blood clots *outside* his brain. They said it is good that there was no intrusive surgery to the brain. He is moving his body parts, which is good since he has an acute c-spine injury. This movement lets us know that he is *not* paralyzed. We are praising God for the little signs. Tomorrow we will be told whether Luke will need surgery on his neck and back (fusing/rods in the backbone).

We have been overwhelmed by the expressions of love and prayers from the body of Christ. It doesn't matter where we go, *His* arms, feet, and mouth are seen through our brothers and sisters in Christ. We have been truly blessed by the outpouring of concern from Luke's boss and the staff where he works. His boss was the one who called us initially to voice his concern about Luke. I praise God that he was led to call us. He said he had debated whether or not to do so since he didn't want to infringe on Luke's privacy. Thank You, Lord, that *You* prompted him so we would be able to find Luke.

It pains us to know that for three days Luke had no one at His side, but I am comforted in knowing that *his Abba Father* had been with him with ministering angels even before Luke arrived at the hospital. God was sustaining him, directing the doctors, comforting Luke's spirit, and being *our* God, *our* Father. We found out through a tech attending to Luke that this hospital has the *best* trauma unit on the West Coast. Praise God! Luke was taken to the best doctors to care for him.

Although we did not feel like eating, we had supper at the restaurant where Luke works. Everyone was so caring. His boss took care of our hotel stay for one week. God has once again provided for our needs. When going to the hotel, both of us so weary—mentally, emotionally and physically— we prayed that God would give us—His beloved—rest! It is very hard to rest when your mind tumbles with thoughts and concerns. Even in that simple prayer, God heard us and actually gave us sleep! "Come to me *all* who are heavy-laden and I *will* give you rest."

· · · · ·

God, help me to praise you in the little things. Thank You for showing me how much You care for me through people's expressions of love. Let me rest in You. Amen.

Reflections

_____

_____

_____

_____

_____

_____

_____

_____

_____

A MOM'S HEART (DAY 3)

Cast your cares on the Lord and he will sustain you; he shall never let the righteous be shaken. —Psalm 55:22

We awoke early (3 a.m.) to get back to the hospital before the horrendous rush hour LA traffic. (Who would ever want to live there? They say that traffic starts getting bad by 4 a.m. What?) We spoke with the doctor, and he is pleased with Luke's progress. He is glad we are here and thinks it is helping Luke.

We asked Luke to lift two fingers and he did. The joy we

8

feel in knowing *he hears us* and that he is responding to our command is overwhelming. He is medicated a lot so he is somewhat limited in his response, but we rejoice in each sign of progress! We were told that the surgery done on his brain was not intrusive. In other words, they operated on the outside of the brain.

My heart aches as I see my son in so much pain. I want to make it all better for him. I want to see him awake with a smile and a joke for me. Luke is so good at making people feel better. He is always ready with a joke or silly story. I want to believe that his squeeze of my hand or eye flutter is a response to me and not involuntary. We have learned to take each little sign of progress as encouragement.

The Lord God, our *Healer* is busy with the "Luke Bernard Assignment." We are praying for *full* restoration even to the point where surgery will not be necessary on his back. The doctor said he fractured the bones, and rods will have to be put in so the bones fuse and the spine is protected. We are believing God is taking care of that fusion without surgery. It is reassuring to know that others are standing with us in prayer, believing for Luke's healing.

• • • • •

Lord, help me to trust You. It's hard to fully trust You in this situation, but I will. Help me to cast all my cares on You. Amen.

Reflections

_____

_____

_____

_____

_____

_____

_____

_____

_____

_____

HE IS MY HEALER! (DAY 3)

This sickness will not end in death. No, it is for God's glory so that God's Son may be glorified through it. —John 11:4

We have been overwhelmed by the response of love, encouragement, and prayers from so many people. So many people we don't even know have responded, but it's the body of Christ in action. Unbelievable! We had three local pastors come today for prayer, with others coming in the next few days. Thank You, Lord, for ministering to us as well as Luke!

The doctors consulted about Luke's back injury and feel

his injury isn't bad enough to need surgery. They feel it will heal on its own, but he might need a brace. *Praise God! He is Luke's Healer!* Thank You, Lord, for hearing our prayers. We are continuing to pray for *full* healing of Luke's back.

The doctor also wanted to start doing command response. Luke is moving his limbs, which is good, but the doctor wanted to see if he would respond to commands. We asked him to lift *one* finger, then *two* fingers, *and he did!* The excitement we felt was so unbelievable because we know he *knows* we are here—he hears us—and he is responding.

One of the many scriptures we have read is the story of Jesus healing Lazarus. John 11:4 says,

> *When he heard this, Jesus said, "This sickness* [or this accident in Luke's case] *will not end in death. No, it is for God's glory so that God's Son may be glorified through it."*

Even now we pray that this accident will not end in death but bring glory to God. Jesus told Mary and Martha that Lazarus would rise again. We are believing the same for Luke Benjamin Bernard.

• • • • •

God, I thank You that You are still a Healer. Lord, help me to believe that You can heal sicknesses, relationships, wounds, and situations in my life. Help me to believe that good can come out of bad situations so that You might get glory. Amen.

Reflections

_____

_____

_____

_____

_____

_____

_____

_____

_____

_____

DON'T GET DISCOURAGED!
(DAY 3)

Don't be afraid, for I am with you. Don't be discouraged,
for I am your God. I will strengthen you and help you. I
will hold you up with my victorious right hand.
—Isaiah 41:10 (NLT)

Luke has swelling in his brain and a broken back. The doctors say that there are no chest or abdominal injuries, which is good news. He is able to breathe on his own. They are also very optimistic about his recovery since he is young and strong. We are very optimistic because we know the power of prayer.

Luke has moved his arms and feet, which means his spinal injuries have not paralyzed him. Today the doctors told us to ask Luke to move his fingers and he responded. They told the nurses, and everyone is very hopeful.

He is still in a lot of pain. The doctors are heavily medicating him for the pain and want his swelling to go down before they lessen the pain meds. However, he seems to be conscious and responding. He knows that we are here. Most importantly, I believe that he knows God is here. We are trusting God to continue to heal him.

We are very concerned with the swelling of his brain. It has to stop swelling and start going down. Then Luke's brain has to handle the pressure once they turn off the drain tube. We are trying not to get discouraged and pray about each little detail that needs to take place for the next thing to happen.

· · · · ·

Lord, please help me not to get discouraged as I walk through this valley. I know You are walking with me and will help me. Help me when I feel afraid and overwhelmed. Amen.

Reflections

_____

_____

_____

_____

_____

_____

_____

_____

_____

IS GOD IN CONTROL? (DAY 4)

Go your way, your faith has made you well.
—Mark 10:52 (NASB)

I was reminded today of the story of Bartimaeus in Mark 10:46-52. He was a blind man sitting by the road. He was told that Jesus was coming and cried out to Him. Jesus asked him, "What do you want me to do for you?" Bartimaeus replied, "I want to see!" Jesus' response was, "Go your way, your faith has made you well," and immediately he was healed.

If Jesus asked that question today I would say, "Heal my son, Luke." We stand on the prayers of faith with thousands praying for Luke's healing. We are believing that Luke *will be healed*. We are praying that healing will be quick and will show God's glory for all to see. God is the same yesterday, today, and forever. He's still in the miracle working business!

• • • • •

God, help me to pray specific prayers about what I need. Help me when I am weak and tired and want to give up. Help me to believe You are working during this difficult time. Amen.

Reflections

_____

_____

_____

_____

_____

_____

_____

_____

_____

_____

HAVE NO FEAR (DAY 4)

God is our refuge and strength, an ever-present help in trouble. Therefore we will not fear." –Psalm 46:1-2

Luke has had a peaceful, quiet day. We found out that yesterday they shut off the tube to his brain. His levels are good. After a CAT scan, they will make the decision to pull the tubes from his head. We are praying for a good report!

They also did another scan of his full body for his other injuries. We continue to believe the good report that they think at this time no surgery will be necessary and healing will come on its own. We are praying that tomorrow will be "goodbye tubes" *to his brain and in his mouth.* He is breathing on his own but needs tubes for suctioning.

They have lessened the pain meds and continue to wean him off the meds, machines, etc. We are praying specifically about the pain as they will start to wake him up after the tubes are gone. God is Luke's "refuge and strength, an ever-present help in trouble, therefore we *will not fear."* He is also *our* refuge, *our* strength as parents, a very present help so we don't have to *fear.* We are grateful for all who are standing with us, praying, believing, and expecting miracles!

• • • • •

God, I turn to You now because I feel weary and weak. Help me to seek refuge in You. Help me to have peace when everything within me is screaming out with fear. I need You, Lord! Amen.

Reflections

_____

_____

_____

_____

_____

_____

_____

_____

_____

_____

PRESSING ON (DAY 5)

Bless the Lord, O my soul and all that is within me, bless His holy name. –Psalm 103:1 (NKJV)

Remember the feeling you experienced when you saw your child walk for the first time? Or how about when they said their first word? Elation or excitement might be what you would say. I was so blessed last night when Luke woke up, opened his eyes a little, and looked at me. Daniel did a voice command: "Luke, if you see your mom, squeeze my hand." He did. Again, "Luke if you see mom, put your hand out flat." He did. We both rejoiced that now he hears and can see us!

This morning they are taking him off meds to fully wake him up and see how he responds to things. We are praying and believing that his mouth tube will come out soon. We do not want a trachea to be put in. Doctors say that it is a standard procedure for injuries like this, *but* we serve a miracle working God. We are praying specifically for the next two days for good progress. They want to do this procedure on Monday.

Doctors also shared with us about diffuse axonal brain injuries. It is when a traumatic injury happens and an individual's head and upper torso are moved back and forth in motion. (The brain moves within the skull.) We will not know what that might mean until Luke is functioning. We are praying specifically that his brain will be healed, and there will be no problems.

We continue to be blessed by so many people with such an outpouring of love, concern, and prayers. Several local pastors have come to pray with us. A couple of praying women also came to encourage us with their prayers. Luke's church and care group have been reaching out to us and blessing us as well. We are overwhelmed by how many are praying and standing with us in this miracle of healing.

I am constantly reminded that God is close to us *all* the time, not just in crisis. He desires to be our friend, our Father, our Savior—whatever we need. He is close to the brokenhearted and the downtrodden, and cares about the details of our lives. But, He is a gentleman and doesn't force a relationship. He simply says, "Come to Me."

• • • • •

Lord, help me to press on as I go through this time. Help me to know You are near to me when I am brokenhearted, downtrodden, upset, or discouraged. Instead of running from You, help me to come to You with all my cares. Amen.

Reflections

_____

_____

_____

_____

_____

_____

_____

_____

_____

_____

GOD IS WORKING
ON OUR BEHALF (DAY 5)

The Lord will fight for you; you need only be still.
—Exodus 14:14

We finished a good day! Luke was off his pain meds for most of the day and was awake. He followed commands and even made us laugh when he started putting up two fingers or a "thumbs up" without any prompting. I think he wants the mouth tube out more than we do. We have explained to him that he has to follow directions enough so that the doctors feel he can spit on command. We are praying and *be-*

lieving that it is coming out by Monday! We are encouraged by countless people who are praying in agreement with us. Each time we ask Luke to do something, it feels like running a marathon. We have been so grateful that he has also been sleeping and resting today. God's perfect peace is surrounding him, and we are seeing a true miracle continue to unfold!

We were blessed to have Luke's Bible study leaders come and share lunch with us. It is such a blessing to meet others who care for Luke and are praying on his behalf. They shared with us that several weeks before the accident, Luke had come to a small group fellowship and shared his struggles. Several had promised to follow up with him but had not. The leaders said the accident hit them hard, and they should have reached out to Luke and tried to minister to him. As a result of the accident, the church put measures in place to help people more effectively.

We also have been so blessed by unbelievable doctors and nurses that care for Luke. This hospital, we are told, is the best on the west coast. We have the best care! Thank you God!

We are also praying for the other nine individuals in the ICU ward. One mother I met has a son who was shot when he was going home from work. Pray for him to recover. I have been able to share and pray with his mom. I'm looking forward to a good day tomorrow!

• • • • •

God, thanking you for working on my behalf. Thank you for encouraging me. Thank you for bringing people to encourage me and pray with me. I love you, Lord. Amen.

Reflections

_____

_____

_____

_____

_____

_____

_____

_____

_____

RESTING IN GOD
(DAY 6)

Rest in the Lord and wait patiently for Him.
–Psalm 37:7 (NKJV)

Today has been quiet, and Luke has rested peacefully all day. It is fitting that today is Sunday—the day of rest. It has been hard for us today because we are extremely tired. I think a week spent with Luke in ICU has caught up with us. We are so grateful to those who prayed during this time for God to renew our strength.

Late in the afternoon, Luke woke up and listened to us talk and even followed some commands. Zach, his Bible study leader from church, came by to bring us lunch. He stayed to visit as we ate lunch, spent time in prayer, and Luke showed what he could do. Joy and Mary, other new friends, came about the same time to visit. We were encouraged by them and had a sweet time of prayer and fellowship. God is so good to know what we need and to bring it at the exact time we need it! The following is one of the passages we have read that has encourage us:

> *Hear my cry, O God; give heed to my prayer. From the end of the earth I call to You when my heart is faint; lead me to the rock that is higher than I. For You have been a refuge for me, a tower of strength against the enemy.*
>
> *Let me dwell in Your tent forever; let me take refuge in the shelter of Your wings. For You have heard my vows, O God; You have given me the inheritance of those who fear Your name. You will prolong the king's* [Luke's] *life; his* [Luke's] *years will be as many generations.*
>
> *He* [Luke] *will abide before God forever; appoint loving- kindness and truth, that they may preserve him. So I will sing praise to Your name forever, that I may pay my vows day by day.* —Psalm 61 (NASB)

Many join us in praying *specific, desperate, unified* prayers. Here is what we are praying:

1. Pray that God continues to heal Luke's brain, back, neck, and face.

2. Pray that we can get tubes out of his mouth without a trachea. The doctors want to fit him with a back brace,

hopefully tomorrow, so they can get him sitting up and see what he can do with breathing, coughing, etc. If he does well, they will not have to do the trachea. I see this as an answer to our prayers, so pray that this will happen tomorrow, and we get a good report!

3. Pray for wisdom and strength for us. We are tired physically, mentally, emotionally, and spiritually.

We are so thankful for all the prayers, encouragement, and help with our other kids, etc. God has truly blessed us through so many who love and care for us and our family. *Keep praying. God is doing a miracle right before our eyes!*

· · · · ·

Hear my cry God. I am tired and feel alone. Help me to keep praying even when I don't feel like it. Help me to believe that You are here and will help me. I'm struggling. Help me! Amen.

Reflections

_____

_____

_____

_____

_____

_____

_____

_____

BE NOT AFRAID (DAY 7)

Be strong and courageous! Do not tremble or be dismayed, for the Lord your God is with you wherever you go.

—Joshua 1:9 (NASB)

When you are confronted with such a dramatic event such as we were, it does test your faith. It grips your heart, and fear can really consume you. In the natural, that is what happens. But what happens if you have the supernatural in play through the God of the universe? How are we supposed to approach it?

The scriptures tell us to "Pray without ceasing"; "Do not tremble or be afraid, for the Lord God is with you"; "Pray without doubting"; and the list of scriptures goes on. The real test is not thinking and feeling in the natural but moving in faith to what His Word says. The Word is powerful and helps in times of trouble. We stand firmly on who God is and what He promises us in His Word. We are walking in *faith*, not doubting, that Luke *will be* healed and have a miraculous testimony of God's mercy and grace. During this time, people have been praying for us to be strong and stand firm. Pray for our family. God's peace has been so present, and Luke's sleep is so peaceful!

Today we moved forward some with a new neck brace,

and a back brace was also put on. With the back brace in place, Luke's bed was raised 30% to see how he does. Tomorrow they will raise him up some more until he is sitting up. When this happens, they can do some airway tests, spitting, etc. to see if he can do it on his own. If not, a temporary trachea will be inserted so he can be more comfortable. Pray that Luke handles this transition well.

We rejoice that he is not on pain medicine (just an amount if needed for slight fever). He is not in pain but resting so peacefully. Pray that we will continue to be encouraged with the small signs of improvement and don't become discouraged. Of course, as parents, we just want him to jump out of bed and come home with us.

Again, we thank so many of you who have lifted us up in prayer. We know all the prayers are being heard. God has provided so much for us through a hotel stay, car rental, place to stay, food, new friends, etc. We are amazed that just when we need something, God answers our prayer immediately.

One item we are working on is getting the power of attorney for Luke so we can handle his personal business. Pray we get a lawyer to do this paperwork so we can proceed with dealing with car insurance, his car, etc. We feel your love, support, encouragement, and prayers! God is faithful!

• • • • •

God, help me to keep what You say in Your Word in front of me and not listen to what I think or what others are speaking to me. Help me to walk in faith and not doubt that You are working. I need You to help me be strong and not be afraid. Amen.

Reflections

_____

_____

_____

_____

_____

_____

_____

_____

_____

_____

12

STANDING IN PRAYER (DAY 8)

In the morning, Lord, you hear my voice; in the morning I lay my requests before you and wait expectantly.

—Psalm 5:3

Luke woke up for about an hour this morning and was responsive to us. We are hoping that this happens again in the late afternoon or evening. We are doing exercises with his legs, feet, and hands to keep his muscles moving while he's in bed. He is now going to the bathroom on his own through a catheter, and I even saw him yawn. All these little movements are good signs of recovery. He is moving his lips as well. They took the back brace off late yesterday so he is 30% elevated in his bed without the brace. He is certainly more comfortable. He is really sweating even though he really doesn't have a temperature. Needless to say, his body is working hard to recover. More awake time is what we want so Friday he won't have to be get the trachea.

We are standing in prayer. God has been faithful to see Luke's condition improve step by step. From the drain pressure subsiding so the drain tube could be removed to the report his two vertebrae fractions would not need surgery. All swollenness has gone down, and his head is almost back to normal size. Even when Luke is under sedation for pain, he is still moving quite a bit. He followed some commands to wiggle his toes and lift his fingers and thumbs.

• • • • •

Lord, thank You for helping me each step of the way. Help me be thankful for the little progress I make each day in my journey. Amen.

Reflections

_____

_____

_____

_____

_____

_____

_____

_____

_____

_____

WAITING IS SO HARD (DAY 8)
(Blog from Daniel)

Wait on the Lord; be of good courage and He shall strengthen your hearts, Wait, I say, on the Lord.

–Psalm 27:14

One day as I held his hand and said, "Luke, I love you. You're my buddy." He rubbed his thumb up and down on my hand in response as if to say, "Dad, I love you." Since we have had so much progress on Saturday with the drain tube being removed, his response to commands, etc., we thought Sunday was going to be a banner day. We thought everyone will be in church praying and Luke will do great, but instead there was no movement. By early afternoon, I was discouraged.

A thought came into my mind that God preserved Luke so I could have this last moment with him. It seemed reasonable, even kind or compassionate, but also bittersweet and second best. God sent two ladies (Joy and Mary) from Calvary Chapel Church to pray with me. I exposed this thought, and they helped me to bring those thoughts captive and obedient to Christ. It seemed like a good thought—it even sounded loving—but it was from the enemy and not God's best for Luke. I repented of entertaining that thought and got back to believing God at His Word.

I believe God is the resurrection and the life. This is who He is, so that is what He can do. He will resurrect Luke and give him life abundantly. I believe regardless of what I see, Luke will be a ministry partner. God has work for him to do, lives that need his joy and life-giving spirit, and his determination to be excellent.

After prayer, I went back into the hospital to Luke's room with Zach (who is Luke's home group leader). We had a good time of prayer, and then Luke opened his eyes. He stayed awake for twenty plus minutes. Luke would look to one side then the other as Zach and I spoke. He was following our voices. Zach and I made several jokes, and Luke was grinning. I could see that he enjoyed hearing comedy and laughter. "A merry heart is like a medicine."

I asked him, "Luke, do you need your rest? Do you want us to keep hanging out with you?" He squeezed my hand the hardest yet. After he followed several commands, he fell asleep. I was flying! God knew the right timing of when I needed encouragement, and God used Luke to give it to me.

• • • • •

God, help me not to get discouraged. Keep my mind on You and what Your Word says and not on what man (doctors, lawyers, family, etc.) might say to me. Amen.

Kathy Bernard

Reflections

_____

_____

_____

_____

_____

_____

_____

_____

_____

14

CAN GOD REALLY MAKE ALL THINGS NEW? (DAY 8)
(Blog from Daniel)

He who was seated on the throne said, "I am making everything new." –Revelation 21:5

The next day Luke was unusually quiet and still. We spoke to him about getting better so we could take the tube out of his mouth. He immediately shot his thumbs up, which made us laugh. Usually it's a slow thumbs up. This time they shot up as if to say, "Get this thing out of my throat."

31

Luke's last couple of days have been less responsive. His vitals are excellent, but there has been very little movement. He is off all but an occasional pain medication. We believe now his body is resting to recover. The doctors need him to wake up and stay awake so they can remove his great nemesis—the breathing tube. We believe God is doing a deep work in Luke, not just physically but also spiritually. God is making all things new.

We believe we will see Luke desire to be focused and purposed to filling God's destiny in his life and truly serve Christ, and that his acting would fit into God's plan not vice versa. The next few days we will see God manifest Himself in Luke—the bearer of light (that is what his name means) and his middle name, Benjamin, the son of my right hand. We are believing he will be able to minister and testify of God's mercy and His might. He will share with those at his work, at the hospital, thousands on Facebook, and in churches and his other social services. Luke will impact thousands for Christ through his testimony of God's work in his life!

My desire is that Luke will serve with me in training and sending young adults on short-term mission trips. I would like for him to put together plays for inner city children and take these plays to other churches. I believe he will help raise funds for the ministry, and through the plays, will see people come to know Christ. Yes, he will do movies, but this will not be his focus. God will bless him with opportunities, but they won't be his focus. I would like him to have a drama/arts school and see his students go on to great achievements, as well as stand for Christ.

• • • • •

Lord, thank You that I can trust You that You are making all things new. I believe You are working all things for my good. Amen.

Reflections

_____

_____

_____

_____

_____

_____

_____

_____

_____

_____

GOD ANSWERS PRAYERS
(DAY 8)

The steps of a good man are ordered by the Lord.
—Psalm 37:23 (NKJV)

Another point of God's faithfulness was when we were told that it would be a significant event to shut off the drain tube. They said if Luke's brain pressure would not go up, they could remove that tube. I can't remember the day, but we asked the nurse, "Is his brain pressure steady enough so you can turn off the drain from his brain?" The nurse looked at me quizzically, "I thought I told you yesterday that we turned it off. He is doing fine." God answered my prayer before we could pray!

The Word of God says, "The steps of a good man are ordered by the Lord." We believe the steps to Luke's complete healing and recovery are ordered by God. We are trying to be sensitive to the steps that God has ordained as Luke walks out his recovery.

• • • • •

Thank You, Lord, for answering my prayers. You are so faithful. I continue to trust in You no matter how I feel or what I think. You are working. Amen.

Reflections

_____

_____

_____

_____

_____

_____

_____

_____

_____

16

STANDING ON THE PROMISES OF YOUR WORD (DAY 9)

Not one word has failed of all the good things that the Lord your God promised concerning you. All have come to pass for you; not one of them has failed. –Joshua 23:14 (ESV)

Most of us can remember growing up and being promised something. Maybe it was Mom saying, "I promise you can have this or do that if you _____." Or maybe it was Dad saying, "I promise this weekend I'll take you to the park." When those promises are made, children cling to them and expect them to happen. Unfortunately, many of us have experienced times of disappointment when that promise was not kept. As I was reflecting about God's promises in His Word, I realized that God has made a lot of promises. What is even more amazing is that He has kept every one He has made. Having that kind of track record, we can boldly believe in those promises and stand on them.

His Word is still alive and active. He wants us to believe in those promises and claim them. It is interesting that just as I am reflecting on the promises of God, our daughter Bethany sent us a song that speaks about the promises of God. It talks about love never failing and that God makes all things work together for our good. Although we may experience pain during the night, joy does come in the morning.

· · · · ·

God help me to believe your promises even when so many people have broken their promises to me. Help me to believe and trust You! Help me to believe that You always keep Your promises. Amen.

Reflections

_____

_____

_____

_____

_____

_____

_____

_____

_____

_____

PEACE THAT SURPASSES ALL UNDERSTANDING (DAY 9)

My soul, wait silently for God alone, for my expectation is from Him. –Psalm 62:5

Luke is not very active right now. I have a peace that God is working and mending him as he sleeps. I believe we need to be patient and wait on God. I have to admit that patiently waiting on God is not an easy thing to do. We are used to instant gratification in our lives and expect results immediately. God can certainly work that way, but sometimes it takes time—days, months or even years. Do I have the strength to endure and wait on God, continuing to believe His promises for our lives?

We are at the point where Luke needs to wake up more so they can see how well he takes commands about breathing deeply. They are hoping that we can get to that point in the next few days where they will not have to continue the plans for a trachea. The tubes can stay in up to two weeks, and then they have to take them out. Two weeks will be Saturday, *so we are praying that we can get over this hurdle!*

· · · · ·

God help me to believe that You are working even when I don't see anything. Help me to be patient as I wait for You to work. Give me Your peace! Amen!

Reflections

_____

_____

_____

_____

_____

_____

_____

_____

_____

_____

Kathy Bernard

GOD, HELP ME PRAISE YOU!
(DAY 13)

Praise God, who did not ignore my prayer or withdraw his unfailing love from me. –Psalm 66:20 (NLT)

We have been very fortunate that with six children we have never had any hospital stays or emergencies until now. Maybe God knows I don't do well with blood, needles, and pain situations. Probably the worst "sick" situations happened when we were missionaries in Nigeria, West Africa, and the kids had malaria.

Needless to say, this experience has been quite an eye opener about hospitals and health care. We have been so fortunate to have some of the best doctors and nurses attending to Luke. We have been blessed with great care over Luke's need and are so grateful. We thank God for all His provisions!

As I pondered today about the blessing of walking in health throughout the years with the kids, thankfulness welled up in my heart. God has been so good to take care of my children. We believe each one is a gift from the Lord, and we are to be good stewards of them while we have them. Our mission has been to train, teach, nurture, and disciple each child to shoot them in the right direction to fulfill the destiny that God has for their lives. As most of you know, raising

39

children is a blessing but can also have its challenges and difficulties. It is during those difficult times that God's peace can help us as a parent.

• • • • •

Lord, thank You for Your goodness. Thank You for Your provision. Help me to find blessings in my life and appreciate them, even when I'm going through this valley. I praise You in the midst of my pain. Amen.

Reflections

_____

_____

_____

_____

_____

_____

_____

_____

_____

_____

THANK YOU FOR YOUR OVER-WHELMING PEACE (DAY 13)

And the peace of God, which transcends all understanding will guard your hearts and your minds in Christ Jesus. – Philippians 4:7

During this time, we have felt *His peace*. How do you explain experiencing God's peace even in tragedy? You can't really understand it, *but* He promises it. That peace guards your heart and mind of wrong thoughts, negative ideas, and doubts and assures you that God is working *all things* for His glory. We have been so blessed to have His peace over this situation.

Luke stayed awake longer today. We are exercising his limbs to keep his muscles from tightening up as a result of lying in bed so long. The tube will come out today, either by the doctors saying he is awake and doing enough commands that they can remove it or by putting in the trachea. We are at peace with whatever decision is made. Many prayers have been prayed, and we know that even at the last minute the doctors can change their minds and not do the procedure.

We continue to pray for Luke's complete healing and restoration. We continue to praise God for His faithfulness—each day we are seeing progress, even if it's very small. And we continue to pray *big* prayers that Luke could wake up and be completely restored in his brain, back, and neck. We praise God for all those who have stood in the gap and are praying prayers of *faith* for Luke!

• • • • •

Thank You, God, for your peace. It is comforting and overwhelming to be going through this dark deep valley and still have a supernatural peace. I love You, God! Amen.

Reflections

_____

_____

_____

_____

_____

_____

_____

_____

_____

CAN THANKSGIVING FEED MY FAITH? (DAY 14)

The Lord has heard my cry for help; the Lord will answer my prayer. –Psalm 6:9

Yesterday it was interesting when we started praying and listing all the ways God has worked from the very beginning of when Luke had the accident until now. The list is *long*, showing God's protection, provisions, and steps of healing. Even before the accident, God was with Luke. And at the accident scene, God was with Luke even before the rescue teams arrived. God was with Luke, bringing him to the best hospital for medical care. God was with Luke through surgery, guiding the surgeons as they removed the blood clots. God was with Luke for three days when we didn't know he was hurt and in the hospital. God was there to guide scores of nurses and doctors in his care and has been here each day to bring progress and stabilization to his health. He is here!

Our thanksgiving to God feeds our faith. Our faith doesn't heal Luke, but our faith *in God* heals. God operates in faith, and then thanksgiving feeds that faith. It is easy to let fear, doubt, or unbelief creep in when the progress that we want to see isn't made. But when we reflect and specifically *thank God* for each thing He has already accomplished, it feeds our faith and encourages us to keep believing and praying for the completion of this miracle in the making.

We rejoiced today to come at 5 a.m. in the morning and find Luke awake. He stayed awake all morning, the longest amount of time thus far. Today we struggled because the doctors told us Luke had to have a trachea inserted. As a mom, I think of Luke having a scar on his throat and wondering how long he would have to have it. Questions filled my head of how this would affect his speech and life. It was an emotional time for us.

In the early afternoon, they did the trachea and repositioned the feeding tube to his nose. Hopefully this will make him a lot more comfortable and help toward his recovery. It is hard for us to see this, but we know it is the best for his recovery right now. Hopefully tomorrow the breathing machine will be taken away, and Luke will be totally stable without any machines. We are rejoicing in all the progress. We continue to pray for a fast recovery, while resting at peace with God's timetable for Luke's recovery. No matter what, I will continue to say, "In *everything* give thanks for this is the will of God."

• • • • •

God help me to be thankful in my crisis even when I'm hurt, paralyzed by fear, and can't hardly function. Let me have a thankful heart even when I struggle to find anything to be thankful for. Amen.

Reflections

_____

_____

_____

_____

_____

_____

_____

_____

_____

_____

PRAYERS BY OTHERS (DAY 15)
(Blog by Luke's sister, Bethany)

First of all, then, I urge that supplications, prayers, intercessions, and thanksgivings be made for all people.

—1 Timothy 2:1 (NRSV)

Recently I have been learning about the power of prayer. I know many times when something wrong happens in our lives, we begin to fervently pray. Sometimes our prayers can be fueled by fear. We begin to desperately seek God out of fear of what might happen or what has happened. But what about when we begin to hear good reports or time passes by so that the fear does not sicken our stomach anymore?

I think when our fear subsides, sometimes our desperation does as well. We begin to place our trust in the doctor's reports, the strength of others, or even our own strength. We begin to think that we can handle this physical and emotional battle on our own. But what we fail to realize is that it is more a spiritual battle than anything else. The minute we begin relying on our own understanding, strength, or faith, we lose the most powerful driving force in our victory—the power of God.

Over and over again, I have seen people fall to their knees before God in dire situations. When things seem to be unbearable or the valley seems too dark, they finally turn to the light. But once God begins to lead them out of the darkness or lifts their load, they begin to think that maybe He did not have anything to do with their circumstances at all. Somehow life just figured itself out. Somehow healing and miracles are just coincidences that take place. But God is intentional. He does not heal someone or bring about a miracle just because. He does it to bring Himself glory. He does it so that person could bring Him glory.

I sometimes allow myself to function out of my own strength and lose sight of where I should look for it. I even allow my trust and reality to depend upon the physical circumstances instead of His unwavering spiritual truth. I also let prayer subside when my fear begins to fade. But I know that God wants us to earnestly seek Him through the good and bad.

He wants us to continually seek His strength even when we think we can handle it on our own. Most of all, He wants us to recognize His hand in our lives and begin to glorify Him through how we live.

• • • • •

Dear God, despite my circumstances and how life treats me, help me to forever remain focused on You. I pray that I never allow my trust to be placed in the things of this world, which are temporary, but in You and Your promises, which are eternal. Amen.

Reflections

_____

_____

_____

_____

_____

_____

_____

_____

_____

_____

22

LORD, ARE YOU FIGHTING FOR ME? (DAY 16)

Do not fear! Stand by and see the salvation of the Lord which He will accomplish for you today.

–Exodus 14:13 (NASB)

When a tragic event hits your life, it is very easy to lose hope, become discouraged, and doubt. It is human nature to have all these emotions. When we are under stress and are weary, we can even begin to question God. Why? It is here that we move from the physical and normal emotions to the supernatural faith that only God, the Father of the Universe, can give. When you are losing hope, He gives *hope*. When there is discouragement, He gives *encouragement*. When there is doubt, we need to have *faith* in Him and His Word.

Today we were reminded of an Old Testament story when the Israelites were leaving Egypt and had reached the Red Sea. Pharaoh decided that letting them go was not a good idea so he pursued them. Needless to say, the Israelites were backed into a corner with no way out. Pharaoh and his army were coming towards them with the Red Sea at their back.

Moses answered the people, "Do not be afraid. Stand firm and you will see the deliverance the Lord will bring you today. The Egyptians you see today you will never see again. The Lord will fight for you; you need only to be still. The Egyptians will know that I am the Lord when I gain glory through Pharaoh, his chariots and his horsemen. (Ex. 14:13-14, 18).

Then what does God do? He provides a miracle for the Israelites and opens up the Red Sea like a wall to them on the right and the left. I thought about how I would feel as I walked through on dry land and saw walls of water on each side of me. I'm sure there was wonder, excitement, and probably some fear that the wall of water would come down on me. Certainly trust had to be present to do what God instructed them to do. After everyone had crossed, Pharaoh and his army started to follow. Then God released the water to come down and the army was destroyed.

And when the Israelites saw the mighty hand of the Lord displayed against the Egyptians, the people feared the Lord and put their trust in him and in Moses his servant (Ex. 14:31).

Luke and our family are walking through an extremely difficult time. God has already showed us His power by saving Luke's life. Now God is telling us not to fear and to stand and see what He will accomplish. He is fighting for us and we can be calm, have hope, be encouraged, and have faith in His Word. We want God to be known and be glorified as He quickens Luke to health and a new life in Him. We want thousands to see our God's great power and through that also believe in the God we serve.

• • • • •

Lord, help me not to fear but to stand on your Word and not the reports of doctors or others. Help me to believe You are working. Give me hope and faith in You. Amen.

Reflections

_____

_____

_____

_____

_____

_____

_____

_____

IN ALL THINGS GIVE THANKS
(DAY 18)
(Blog from Daniel—Part 1)

In everything give thanks for this is the will of God in Christ Jesus for you. —1 Thessalonians 5:18 (NKJV)

Luke rested all day yesterday. We could tell that he was sleeping more restfully without the tubes in his mouth. As parents, we want to see a quick recovery but realize that the rest days are part of the healing process. Today Luke is moving a lot and not having to have help with suctioning him. We are hoping they will take the final tubes away by tomorrow. The only tube he will have then is a feeding tube, which they want to put in his stomach as opposed to up his nose where it is now. We are praying for a quickening of health in his body with full recovery. We are thankful for all those standing in agreement and praying that prayer with us. We are thankful for *all* God has done.

- We are thankful that angels were encamping around Luke when the accident occurred. Luke hit a tree on the passenger side, then went over a fire hydrant before slamming into a tree. The other two hits slowed him down and made it possible for him to live.

- Thank God someone drove by and called for help.
- Thank God the emergency teams got to him and brought him to the USC Medical Center, the best trauma hospital on the west coast, we are told.
- Thank God the two blood clots were outside the brain and *not* inside.
- Thank the Lord for sending Dr. Mahta, regarded as one of the top neurosurgeons, to do the surgery.
- Thank God that angels were ministering to Luke for three days when he was alone in ICU.
- We are thankful for Luke's boss and his concern to call us and tell us he believed something was wrong because Luke never missed work.
- Thank God we were able to call around and eventually locate Luke. Praise God we located him before I got on the plane from Houston to Tampa and could re-route and get to LA more quickly.
- Thank God for moving on Pierre at Southwest Airlines to give me a huge break on re-routing my flight and then bumping me to first class. I am glad because there were far fewer people to give an explanation to as to why I was crying.

• • • • •

Thank you, Lord, for the little things You are doing in my life. I get so overwhelmed by the valley, I don't stop and thank You for what You have already done. Help me, God, when I struggle to have a thankful heart. Amen.

Reflections

_____

_____

_____

_____

_____

_____

_____

_____

_____

_____

I CHOOSE TO PRAISE YOU!
(DAY 2)
(Blog from Daniel—Part 2)

You have been my refuge, a place of safety when I am in distress. O my Strength, to you I sing praises...the God who shows me unfailing love. –Psalm 59:16-17 (NLT)

I continue to lift up my praise and thankfulness for what God has done. I know it is easy to look at what still needs to happen and change so much so that we forget to thank Him for what has already been accomplished.

- Thank You for my not getting lost in LA when I arrived at 1 a.m. in the morning to head to the hospital.

- Thank You, after reading and praying over Luke for several hours that first day, he made his first movements with his arms and legs. My heart leaped as I realized he would not be paralyzed. The doctor told us he had two spinal injuries that would require surgery. The sign on one of the machines read: Do not turn—patient acute spinal injury.

- We thank God for hearing our prayers about his back/neck injuries. Later the doctor said he would not need surgery. They believe it will repair on its own, and Luke will only need a brace. They put the brace on him but later removed it. God, You are awesome! Praying for full recovery of his back and neck.

- The next critical prayer point was to see the swelling go down in Luke's brain. It did! Thank You, Jesus! The pressure on the brain had to subside. After several days of our praying, the pressure seemed to stabilize, and they decided they were going to shut off the drain tube to the brain. The next day I was preparing everyone to pray that the pressure would not go up once the tube was turned off. The next morning I asked the nurse if he thought Luke was doing well enough to turn off the drain. The nurse said, "I thought I told you. We turned if off yesterday and he is doing fine." Wow, you answered, God, before I called out to You! You knew Luke's need before I asked.

- The next day the neurosurgeon took the drainage tube out of his brain. Luke then opened his eyes and began to respond to commands right when we needed encouragement. Thank You, Lord!

- We prayed and hoped the steps of healing for Luke would not require him to have a trachea. His recovery was not fast enough and the trachea was necessary. Praise God the simple procedure was successful. Luke is so relaxed without the tubes in his mouth.

- Luke was sleeping the next 2-1/2 days, recovering from the trachea procedure. I have to admit this is when I lost it. I was so overwhelmed by emotions that I simply wept. I think everything finally caught up with me and I broke. We were frustrated because up to that time Luke was gradually staying awake one hour, then more, up to 3-1/2 hours. Did he digress? His sleep was so deep, his muscles more relaxed. Even then in my grief and overwhelming emotion, I had to still praise God. The third day we walked in, and Luke was moving his arms and legs. That day they took him off the ventilator and now he is breathing on his own. Thank You, God, for Your continued answer to prayers.

- Thank the Lord—no machines, no drips, no medications. His temperature and blood pressure are now normal. He is stable and hopefully he can get out of ICU soon.

· · · · ·

God, thank You for being my refuge and strength. Thank You for helping me go on when I can't function and I am emotionally spent. Thank You for Your unfailing love. You are a good God! Amen.

Reflections

_____

_____

_____

_____

_____

_____

_____

_____

_____

_____

25

I CRY FOR HELP (DAY 18)

The Lord has heard my cry for help; the Lord will answer my prayer. –Psalm 6:9 (NCV)

There is something about *breath* or spirit that brings *life*. God is the life giving spirit. Luke is the temple of the Holy Spirit. His temple was bought by the blood of Christ. God alone has the authority over his body, and He gave us the power to execute that authority on earth. I thank God that people in South America, Nigeria, West Africa, Berlin, and so many across the US, both those who know us and those who don't, are exercising that authority and praying for Luke's healing. We praise God for the body of Christ. We have been encouraged by so many prayers. Please continue to pray, especially in the next procedure to put his feeding tube in his stomach and remove it from his nose. We know this will make him more comfortable. Pray God continues to heal his brain and gives back *all* his functions, memory, etc.

We are not through with this miracle. Luke has still many steps to go. As we thank God for what He has already done, our faith grows stronger in what He will still do. He will complete the work He has started. Thank You, God!

• • • • •

Thank You for Your spirit that gives life. Thank You that Your Holy Spirit gives life, comfort, encouragement—all that I need when I need it. Let me rely on You for help and allow others to help me in my time of need. Amen.

Reflections

_____

_____

_____

_____

_____

_____

_____

_____

_____

26
HEALING CAN'T BE PUT IN A BOX (DAY 20)

Heal me, O Lord, and I will be healed; Save me and I will be saved, for you are the one I praise. –Jeremiah 17:14

It is interesting to see the different ways Jesus healed. The Bible says He healed immediately or suddenly. And then there were healings when Jesus waited before He did something. I think Jesus did it that way so we wouldn't "box" Him into a certain pattern for healing. He can do whatever He wants, however He chooses to heal. Of course our human nature is to want the healing immediately. Or we figure in our minds how that healing will look. No matter what kind of healing we want, when we want it, or how it looks, we can be confident of one thing—He hears our prayers and answers them.

We know that God is healing Luke now. We have seen His hand in His continued process of renewing Luke's health. We are continuing in prayer for that healing to come to completion with Luke renewed physically, mentally, emotionally, and spiritually. We believe God is healing more than just his hurt body—his soul, his inner man.

I have to say that praying for healing is a faith walk. Sometimes we put expectations on God as well as on our timing instead of His timing. He is growing us in patience to wait on Him. It reminds me of a song I taught my kids when they were young. It went like this:

Be patient, be patient don't be in such a hurry.
When you get impatient, you only start to worry,
Remember, remember that God is patient too.
And think about the times when others had to wait for you.

We are taking one day at a time and praying for patience as God does His work on our son. I have learned that if I start thinking about the future, fear and worry can start to creep in. Waiting on God is easy to say but difficult to do. We must learn to be totally dependent on Him not only in the midst of a crisis but also in our normal everyday lives. That is what God desires in His relationship with us. Pray we can learn the lessons He wants to teach Daniel and myself, and even Luke in the coming days in rehab.

The tube is being placed in Luke's stomach. Please pray that the next two days things will be okay, and he will get out of ICU. We were so encouraged with so much activity today. Luke was lifting one arm to his head and touching his face, lifting it up and touching our faces and arms, and putting his hand through our hair. It was comforting to us that he was showing us he cares about us even without speaking anything. Please continue to pray. We feel all your prayers and see the prayers being answered.

· · · · ·

God, help me to be patient as I go through this valley. Let me not think in a box of how You can or will work. Help me to trust Your timing and that You are working on my behalf. Amen.

Reflections

_____

_____

_____

_____

_____

_____

_____

_____

_____

CAN A MOUNTAIN BE THROWN INTO THE SEA? (DAY 24)

(Blog from Daniel)

Have faith in God. Truly I say to you, whoever says to this mountain, "Be taken up and cast into the sea," and does not doubt in his heart, but believes that what he says is going to happen, it will be granted him.

—Mark 11:22-23 (NASB)

I was explaining and praying Mark 11:22-24 to Luke today when God spoke to my heart. The Scripture says,

And Jesus answered them, "Have faith in God. Truly, I say to you [when Jesus says "Truly" this means you can take it to the bank…it's good], *whoever* [that includes all of us] *says to this mountain, 'Be taken up and cast into the sea' and does not doubt in his heart, but believes that what he says will come to pass, it will be done for him.* [Jesus stresses his point by telling us again to pray and ask. It appears He really wants us to do this.] *Therefore, I tell you, whatever you ask in prayer, believe that you have received it, and it will be yours"* (ESV).

God said to me, "I am the ocean." I get it! Have faith in God because God is the ocean that you throw your mountain into. Jesus is not merely speaking in metaphors here. He is telling us to have faith in Him. He says, "I am the ocean. The mountain is big but the ocean is way bigger than any mountain. Take your problem and cast it on Me. I am an ocean of love, mercy, compassion, power and strength." Believe that God is big enough to swallow your mountain whole. I cast this problem onto You, God, and believe I will not see it again. It is swallowed up by the ocean of Your love.

With this new revelation of scripture, I prayed: "Right now I cast into the sea (my God) the total recovery of Luke Benjamin Bernard. I know, like the ocean, it is bigger than the mountain—You are bigger than this problem. You told us to cast it onto You and believe it is done, and it shall be granted unto us. God, according to Your Word, Luke's total recovery is done in Jesus' name. Thank You for being way bigger than any mountain. Thank You for imparting faith to believe. We receive it!"

• • • • •

Help me, God, to have faith in what You can do. My valley is so dark, and I can't see how things can change, but I believe. I cast my mountain into the sea! Amen.

Reflections

_____

_____

_____

_____

_____

_____

_____

_____

_____

DAYS OF TRANSITION (DAY 24)

Wait on the Lord; be of good courage, and He shall strengthen your heart. Wait, I say, on the Lord!

–Psalm 27:14 (NKJV)

The last couple of days have been days of transition. Luke is moving more now, and we have to be right beside him when we unlatch the restraints. We want him to be moving his limbs, but it puts more pressure on us to keep him from doing something that might harm himself (i.e. pulling out tubes, etc.).

A touching moment came when we showed our family picture to Luke. He took it, held it in his hand, and looked at it. Then he put it to his mouth like he was kissing the picture. It deeply touched our hearts!

Friday, I flew home to Florida to be with the other kids. As I sat on the airplane, I struggled with wanting to be there to support my exhausted husband and needy son but know I need to be home to minister to our other kids who are going through this difficult time without us present. All I could do was cry out for strength to God.

Saturday was a good day—the tube came out of Luke's nose *and* he was finally moved out of ICU after three weeks. It is a milestone in Luke's recovery. We rejoice in what God has already done and wait expectantly each day to see what He is going to do.

• • • • •

Lord, help me to wait on You! Help me believe You are working on my valley. Give me strength to go on when I want to quit and give up. Help me to realize that my situation might have some transitions and not be too tough on myself or others. I need You, Lord! Amen.

Reflections

_____

_____

_____

_____

_____

_____

_____

_____

_____

IN AN INSTANT (DAY 24)

I will keep watch for you, my strength, because God is my stronghold. –Psalm 59:9 (HCSB)

We are excited about what God is doing in Luke's life. Yesterday we jumped another hurdle in getting him into a rehab center. The last couple of days have been very difficult, waiting in the hospital for the rehab to open up. They couldn't do much more for him in the hospital, which made him very upset. While he is in rehab, they will really work on all areas (i.e. physical, mental, speech) to get him to recover ASAP. We are praying that his back and neck injuries have been or will be healed. He is doing things that make us think that he is healed.

Pray as we meet with the doctors today about his rehab program. Pray that we have strength and wisdom for this next step of his recovery. Pray that Luke has full recovery of all bodily functions and mentally recovers. Pray that in the next couple of days, the trachea and stomach tube can come out, and he can be eating on his own. He is talking now even though the trachea is in.

Several months ago, I wrote a poem after a dear friend received some terrible news about her granddaughter. I was reminded of it since we have really felt the pain and suffering of tragedy personally through Luke's accident. I added a line about us. "In an Instant" makes us reflect that our lives can change drastically at any moment. We need to be ready and have no regrets in life. We need to love unconditionally, forgive freely, listen closely, have a commitment to Jesus, know our eternal destiny, and live with *no regrets*.

God offers all of this to us freely. We only have to accept His *love and forgiveness*, and desire to follow Him. I know we would not be able to walk this journey without Him by our side.

IN AN INSTANT

You can have all your investments secure
But in an instant the market changes
    and you lose everything.
You can have your life planned out
But in an instant you can find out you have a terminal illness.
You can have indescribable joy at holding a newborn
But in an instant hear the words that child is dying.
You can enter a friendship and think you know that person
And in an instant they can turn on you
    with harsh actions and words.
You can be hugging your child in the morning
And in an instant you can feel unbearable pain as that
    child is taken tragically from you.
One moment you can be healthy
And in an instant you can be in an accident
    fighting for your life.
You can think your marriage is good
And in an instant find out your spouse is cheating on you.
You can feel a deep sense of accomplishment

And in an instant feel despair at losing your job.
Your life can be falling apart
But in an instant Jesus Christ can take and transform you.
In an instant…

• • • • •

*Lord, help me not to dwell so much on my valley that I
don't continue to love unconditionally, forgive freely, and
live my life for You. I don't want any regrets. Help me,
God, in this journey! Amen.*

Reflections

_____

_____

_____

_____

_____

_____

_____

_____

_____

_____

30
HE'S A MIRACLE WORKING GOD
(DAY 27)

With God we will gain the victory. –Psalm 60:12

I continue to be amazed at how God continues to encourage us through His Word. Several verses from Psalms
77:11-14 boosted my spirit during my quiet time.

> *I will remember the deeds of the Lord; yes, I will re-
> member your miracles of long ago. I will consider all your
> works and meditate on all your mighty deeds. Your ways,
> God, are holy. What god is as great as our God? You are
> the God who performs miracles; you display your power
> among the peoples.*

We have reflected on many of the stories in the Bible and
how God performed a miracle to save a nation, bring victory
in a battle, heal people, and drastically save someone from
their sins. As we reflect on these stories, it boosts our faith.
God is the same yesterday, today, and forever. So, if God did
all these miracles in the Bible, can He not do the same *today*?
The answer is *yes!* He is living and active and in the business
of miracles. He has the power to perform miracles. He is a
great God worthy of our praise.

One song we have sung, especially during the first few

days in ICU talks about how He's a miracle working God. Today is one month since Luke's accident. We have seen God at work, performing a miracle of healing Luke. Each step of the way, we have been encouraged with progress. We are still praying and believing God to heal Luke's back and neck so he won't have to wear braces. Please pray in agreement with us that as they re-test him to assess his condition, they will say there are no breaks (he has been healed!), and he can have more freedom to move.

We are now in rehab. *Yes!* He will work with different therapy staff. Yesterday he walked quite a distance with assistance. Then we put him in a wheelchair, and he wheeled himself around with assistance. We encouraged him by timing him going around the unit, and he beat his previous time! Then he went to the physical therapy room where they have different machines for exercise. He walked over to the leg press two times, got on it, and did a couple of leg presses. Yep, he remembers those exercise days at LA Fitness!! He is writing a few words and talking quite a bit. Yesterday he went from mouthing a few words to saying sentences. Not everything makes sense, but he is improving!

Other prayer concerns: Pray the speech therapists release Luke to start eating some liquid stuff. They want to make sure he is swallowing correctly so food doesn't go to his lungs. When he is able to do this, they can take the stomach tube out. Today they changed out the trachea to a different one that will give him more room to swallow and breathe. Then they can cap the trachea and he will talk like normal. Pray that we can move forward in this area. Continue to pray for quick recovery in rehab. They say they will move forward as quickly as Luke wants to. Tuesday all the staff will meet to discuss each area of Luke's program and where we need to go in this recovery. Pray for wisdom and that they will be led by God. We know they can make their plans, but God is still in control of this miracle and *anything* can happen with God. We are believing we can bring Luke home by the end of the month.

• • • • •

God, I thank You that You are a miracle working God! I believe You worked miracles in the past, and You can do the same today. You are in control of my miracle and anything can happen. I praise You. You're a good God. Amen.

Reflections

_____

_____

_____

_____

_____

_____

_____

_____

_____

_____

31

IS GOD'S WORD TRUE? (DAY 30)

Be strong and courageous. Do not be afraid or terrified be-cause of them, for the Lord your God goes with you; he will never leave you nor forsake you. –Deuteronomy 31:6

Each day God knows exactly what we need from His Word. It is living and active and useful for our daily lives. In the verse above, God says to be strong and courageous. How can we do that when we are faced with the most difficult situation we ever faced? It is natural to be exhausted and struggling with one's feelings. It is natural to be fearful of what is going to happen. But God says He will go with us. That is how we can be strong and courageous. He promises to never leave or forsake us. He is with us through the dark uncertain hours and also in those times of rejoicing.

It is interesting that when someone repeats themselves, it usually tells you that it is important. So God is letting us know, *this is important*, so don't be afraid and discouraged! He is the One going before us and walking beside us, and yes, even at times holding us because we simply can't walk. He is giving us everything we need so we don't have to be afraid or discouraged.

This journey has not been an easy one. But as we reflect where we have come in one month, we stand in awe of our

God and His mercy, faithfulness, and healing hand. Luke is a miracle. He continues to improve each day. Today was special just in the fact that he smiled, had a shine in his eyes, and even made us laugh with a joke. That's our Luke! Tomorrow the team meets to evaluate Luke's progress and see when they might release him. They will probably say 3-4 weeks, but with a brain injury the progress can move quite quickly. We are praying that God will move the process along quickly so we can bring him home. Continue to pray that this week we can get him eating food and get the stomach and trachea tubes out. (His trachea is now capped so his voice sounds like himself.) These are the next big steps to recovery.

Pray that each day he will have more and more strength to do all the rehab that they ask of him. Pray for strength for us. We are blessed that we are now staying five minutes from the rehab center. This gives us flexibility to go back and forth if needed. The rehab center provides apartments that are cheap and close to the center. Pray for our other kids that God will give them strength, courage, and encouragement as we are separated from them.

• • • • •

Lord, help to me strong and courageous. I am weak and scared to death. Help me to know Your Word and what You say to me and not base everything on my emotions. Help me to know You are with me and won't forsake me. Amen.

Reflections

_____

_____

_____

_____

_____

_____

_____

_____

_____

COUNTING MY BLESSINGS, NAMING THEM ONE BY ONE
(DAY 31)

Praise God, who did not ignore my prayer or withdraw his unfailing love from me. –Psalm 66:20 (NLT)

When I was a little girl, I used to sing a hymn at church that went like this:

Count your blessings name them one by one.
Count your blessings see what God has done.
Count your blessings, name them one by one.
Count your many blessing see what God has done.

Many times we get caught up with life and the worries and concerns that we don't stop and think about the blessings. Many days we have finished by reflecting about what we can be thankful for. It might be one little thing, but it is a blessing because we are one step closer to recovery.

Today we are counting many blessings. The tests came back regarding Luke's back and neck, saying that they are stable—in other words, they cannot find any breaks! We are praying that tomorrow the group of doctors have decided that braces won't be necessary in the continual recovery process. Luke *hates* to wear the braces. He is conforming to wearing the helmet. I think he realizes that it is for the safety of his head. We have been praying for complete healing of his back and neck. Count your blessings!

We had our food test today. They put little sensors on his neck to help him swallow. He drank some apple juice and ate some pudding! Yea! He said the juice was too sweet. Tomorrow they will continue with this process to get him to eat more and more and not have problems swallowing. He can swallow better now because they changed his trachea to a smaller one and capped it. His voice sounds normal now. Pray specifically that he can be successful so the stomach tube will come out soon. Count your blessings!

The next and last thing to be removed will be the trachea. He also had a successful shower time. Yes, with Daniel's help (Luke did not want the nurses to help), he took a sit-down shower. He loved having the hot water go down his head. That only led to a long comfortable nap! Count your blessings!

• • • • •

Kathy Bernard

God, help me to count my blessings. I struggle to find anything good through this dark time. Help me find something I can appreciate and be thankful for it. Amen.

Reflections

_____

_____

_____

_____

_____

_____

_____

_____

_____

_____

CASTING ALL MY CARES ON YOU (DAY 31)

Cast all your anxiety on him because he cares for you.
—1 Peter 5:7

Pray for Luke's mental recovery. He is slowly putting together his memory. It is a process and can be frustrating for him and his caregivers. We have had some tender moments of sharing and praying together. We are praying for full memory to be restored. We are being educated in injuries like this, and there are eight levels that a patient usually goes through. We are at the four to five level. How fast each level is finished is really up to the patient and how quickly they can progress. They have given us a tentative date of leaving the rehab center as April 27th. We are praying that God will speed up that process, and we will be home sooner. Luke has come a long way in just a month, so we are counting our blessings!

One thing we are beginning to pray about is how we will get Luke home. We are checking with the airlines to see if we can get a direct flight from LA to Tampa. It is a long journey. Pray that doors will open up in the safest and best way to get Luke home. We don't know anyone with a private plane, but that might be an option too. We know God is faithful and will provide for our needs when we need them met. Join us in prayer for this upcoming need. We are so blessed!

One doctor continues to speak out each time he sees Luke, "You are a miracle!" And he is. We are truly counting our blessings!

• • • • •

God, I look to You, I won't be overwhelmed. Give me eyes to see things like You do. God, I look to You. You're where my help comes from. Give me wisdom and trust that You know just what to do for me. Amen.

Reflections

_____

_____

_____

_____

_____

_____

_____

_____

_____

_____

34

GOD, DO YOU HAVE A PLAN?
(DAY 32)

"For I know the plans I have for you," declares the Lord, "plans to prosper you and not to harm you, plans to give you hope and a future." –Jeremiah 29:11

We truly believe that God has a plan for Luke's life. Yesterday we went to get his belongings out of his car. Both Daniel and I could only shake our heads and say, "God you are so good!" His battered car makes you wonder how anyone could have survived the accident. *But*...Luke did! Through this journey, we have continued to see God's hand in preserving Luke's life throughout the accident, surgery, and recovery. Why? Because God has a plan for his life. His purpose—his mission—is still not complete. God is giving Luke a hope and a future!

We are playing games with Luke and he is winning—checkers, Connect 4, etc. He is exercising on some of the machines, walking, communicating more and more, and giving us lots of smiles and even some jokes. It makes us happy to see our Luke come back to us. We are hoping that he will be eating on his own by next week. He continues to amaze us and each day does more things.

Pray he continues to get his memory back and that he is

patient in this process. It is a chore for him to remember things. Pray he continues to improve, and we can bring Luke home by the end of the month. We are believing it will be sooner. Pray for the details of how we will get him home—whether by private plane or direct flight. Our plan is for me to go home the end of next week to get things ready, as well as care for our other children and other business. Daniel will follow with Luke, hopefully in a week to a week and a half. It is a long trip so we are concerned about Luke's safety and strength. Pray that God will provide the best way for him to get home. I am checking with different agencies to see if it is possible to get a flight through them.

We are excited about what God has planned for Luke. He has a platform to share his testimony and his talent. Pray that God will show him clearly what he needs to do. We are also praying now for his surgery in the future to re-construct his skull. They say that will happen in six months to a year. Keep praying.

• • • • •

I know you have a plan for my life. Help me believe that You have a plan for all those I love. God help me to complete Your plan for my life and know that You use all my failures, hurts, and successes for Your glory. Amen.

Reflections

_____

_____

_____

_____

_____

_____

_____

_____

_____

HELP ME TO LIVE
WITH NO REGRETS (DAY 35)

Trust in the Lord with all your heart and lean not on your own understanding; in all your ways submit to him and he will make your paths straight. –Proverbs 3:5-6

Luke is improving each day. We take one day at a time and thank God for each step of improvement. Luke is walking pretty far without assistance. He cycled on the bike today for ten minutes. He plays games and many times wins. He is very competitive. He is doing great with the swallow tests, eating pudding and even an ice cream sandwich. *Yes!* We are getting closer to the stomach tube coming out and freedom from rehab in California.

Today we celebrate five weeks from the time the accident happened. It is hard to believe how much has happened in such a short amount of time. God is an amazing God and still performs miracles. Luke is a walking miracle! It has made me ponder about life and relationships. You never know what might happen in an instant. For that reason, we need to make sure that our relationships are intact. We don't want to live with any regrets, such as, Did I say what I needed to say? Did I forgive that person or appreciate that individual? Did I say, "I'm sorry" or "I love you" and try to make a difference with my life?

When we walk in the moment and don't wait, then we don't run the risk of living with regrets. Jesus even shared about this when He said that we should go and work things out with someone before going to worship Him. I encourage you if you need to correct a relationship to do so.

• • • • •

Lord, help me to not live with regrets. Show me someone or a situation that I need to correct. Help me to walk in love and forgiveness and leave the results to You. Amen.

Reflections

_____

_____

_____

_____

_____

_____

_____

_____

_____

36

GOD HAS BEEN WORKING THE ENTIRE TIME (DAY 37)

The Lord has heard my cry for mercy; the Lord accepts my prayer. –Psalm 6:9

I am going to give a review of this miracle story of Luke Benjamin Bernard. Luke's miracle started the night of the accident. Police term the accident as a possible fatal accident. By looking at the car, you can only shake your head and say, "God saved his life." Not many people walk away from such a severe crash. Luke was taken to the best trauma unit on the

Kathy Bernard

west coast and the best doctor performed surgery on him.

Then there were the three weeks of ICU care with each day more tubes being taken away, his recognition of us by squeezing our hand, wiggling his toes, and finally looking at us and following us with his eyes. Next we went to a hospital room that Daniel would tell you was "hell on earth" because the nurses were not caring for Luke. Daniel became his nurse, advocate, and protector. Finally we were moved to rehab.

In rehab we have had the help of many people assisting Luke with physical and mental therapy. Luke can walk by himself. He exercised ten minutes on the bike the other day. He can take a shower (with supervision), go to the bathroom, brush his teeth, and he even shaved today. He can play some games and is learning to remember basic skills. He is doing well with his food tests and eating pudding, apple sauce, and even an ice cream sandwich! The goal by the end of this week is for him to be eating food with no more stomach tube and trachea. We are excited! The end of the tubes is close.

• • • • •

God, thank You for the miracles You do in my life every day. I am sorry for the miracles and healings that have taken place in my life that I took for granted or did not give You the glory for. I want to praise You in all circumstances and I want my life to bring You glory. Please give me Your strength, peace, faith, and joy to remain steadfast and continue this journey set before me. Amen.

Reflections

_____

_____

_____

_____

_____

_____

_____

_____

_____

_____

37

FITTING THE PIECES TOGETHER (DAY 37)

Yes, my soul, find rest in God; my hope comes from him. –Psalm 62:5

Luke's greatest challenge now is his memory. Each day he improves, but we are learning to be patient. This situation reminds me of a puzzle. It takes time to match the colors, look at the shapes, and complete it. Luke is forming his memories again. It is a struggle because what he thinks might not come out of his mouth. He goes from one thought to another, and many times it doesn't make sense. He works on his memory by doing games and other activities. We had him tested again at the rehab center and everything came back as stable. One of the doctors came today to test all his functions, and he passed with flying colors. I told the doctor after the test that we believe in doctors, but we believe in prayer and that God can heal. He didn't respond, but I believe that God has healed Luke's back and neck. Yes, another miracle!

We are still praying for full recovery. We are hoping by the end of the month to bring Luke home to continue in his recovery, however long it takes. With brain injuries, the recovery can be fast or slow. God is in control and will give us what we need to complete this journey. Pray that in the next two weeks Luke will continue to recover at a fast speed and be ready to go home. The miracle continues, and we are thankful for a God who is so faithful!

• • • • •

Lord, help me to be patient as You take me through this valley. Help to believe that You are in control and working all things for my good. Give me hope for the future. Amen.

Reflections

_____

_____

_____

_____

_____

_____
_____
_____
_____
_____

38
GOD IS NOT FINISHED YET!
(DAY 38)

Praise be to God, who has not rejected my prayer or with-held his love from me!. –Psalm 66:20

This is my last night in the rehab center as I plan to go home and be with our other children and prepare for Luke's homecoming. As I look down on Luke's sleeping face, I am filled with so much thanksgiving for what God has accomplished in five weeks. We serve a miracle working God who cares for us so deeply. I struggle in leaving him again, but I'm glad I have a wonderful husband who is here until the end. Being together through this journey has helped us to strengthen and encourage each other.

We have the date to check out of here as April 30th. We realize that in the next two weeks much can take place. We want Luke to be as healthy in all areas as possible before travelling. We are hoping that next week he will be on a regular food diet. He is working hard on his skills and memory. It takes time and patience with all of us helping him. We are still praying *big* prayers that God will restore Luke completely. We are taking one day at a time and know that God is not finished yet!

Pray for us as we enter these last weeks of rehab here and prepare for the next step. We need wisdom as we seek help in continuing his rehab in Florida. Pray we get favor with a good rehab center that can help him. Pray for our family as we adjust to his needs and learn how to minister to him with love and patience. Pray that Luke will stay encouraged and protect his mind and heart from getting depressed about his injury. Pray as we check on flights for coming home. We want to get a direct flight to make it as easy as possible.

We appreciate all the new friends we have made while here…people who visited and prayed with us, those who brought food, others who took us into their home and extended hospitality to us. We had others who visited Luke—friends from church and work. Many thanks to his boss who initially called us that Luke was missing and then put us up in a hotel for a week and gave us some wonderful meals at his restaurant. Thanks to those who helped us move Luke and the church who stored his personal things. And we couldn't forget all the many doctors and nurses who have helped Luke recover from this accident. We have been truly blessed and taken care of by so many precious people. We are forever grateful. We pray that just as this miracle of healing has unfolded for us, it has been a blessing and encouragement to others who have experienced it and seen God's work. But…*God is not finished yet!*

I will continue to blog as Daniel gives me updates. Please pray for him that he will not get weary but will stay encouraged. It has been a long time, almost two months, with him by Luke's side.

We appreciate the texts, calls, emails, and cards that have encouraged all of us. Pray for me as I fly home tomorrow for safety and wisdom to care for our other children as we prepare for Luke to come home. Please continue to pray specifically for these needs. We are not out of the woods yet and still need many prayers for continued healing and restoration.

· · · · ·

God, I know You have brought me through this valley. I praise You for Your love and never giving up on me and this situation. I know I'm still in great need of You, but I rest in You for the end results. Amen.

Reflections

_____

_____

_____

_____

_____

_____

_____

_____

_____

_____

39

IS ANYONE STANDING IN THE GAP FOR US? (DAY 42)

We do not know how to pray as we should, but the Spirit Himself intercedes for us with groanings too deep for words. –Romans 8:26 (NASB)

I have always liked the story of Nehemiah who returned to rebuild the city walls of Jerusalem. It was a difficult job and he had much opposition. He needed help in many areas to accomplish this task. One job he had was for individuals to stand in the gaps of the wall to protect the city while the walls were being completed. Thus, we have the term today when people ask for prayer they might say, "Will you stand in the gap for me?" Another way of saying this would be, "Will you stand with me in faith during this difficult time?" We have appreciated the thousands who have stood in the gap for Luke and our family the past five weeks. God has used many of you to help us storm heaven's gates for Luke's healing. *God has heard our prayers* and each day is faithfully answering them one by one. It is truly amazing to be witnessing a miracle taking place right before our eyes!

There is much to report since I left Los Angeles late Thursday to head home. Friday, Luke started on solid food and is eating everything in sight. The doctor said that on the first of the week, the stomach tube will come out, closely followed by the removal of the trachea! Friday, Luke also participated in the Walk for Brain Injury that takes place on the rehab campus. It is a one mile walk, and all the patients are encouraged to participate by walking or wheeling in their wheelchairs. Luke walked with two friends from his workplace. He walked about 2/3 of the way and continues to get stronger each day.

He is also getting his memory back more and more. Bethany and I skyped with him today and were truly blessed as Luke is starting to testify of his healing. He is thankful too for the many who prayed for him. We continue to pray for full recovery in all areas. Please continue to stand in the gap as we continue to see this miracle unfold.

His check out date from rehab is April 30th. We are praying for the best way to get Luke home and trusting God for His provisions. At this time we are thinking we will try to get a direct flight and put Daniel and Luke in business class to have more room for Luke to rest. Let us know if you have any resources. We have checked out several special flight companies but we don't fit the requirements. *Thanks for standing in the gap…*

• • • • •

Lord, thank You for those who are standing with me in prayer through my valley. Even when I don't know what to pray, You know my pain and bring me what I need. Help me to pray even when I don't know what to say or feel like doing it. Thank You for listening to me. Amen.

Reflections

_____

_____

_____

_____

_____

_____

_____

_____

_____

40

COMING HOME (DAY 45)

Even though I walk through the darkest valley, I will fear no evil, for you are with me; your rod and your staff, they comfort me. –Psalm 23:4

We have reached several other milestones in Luke's recovery. Yesterday the stomach tube came out, and today the trachea finally, yes, finally came out. *He is tubeless!* After 5 1/2 weeks of tubes, Luke is *free!* We are rejoicing in his recovery.

And…Daniel and Luke are coming home Sunday morning. The doctors have released Luke early so they can leave on Saturday. We found a direct flight on Delta where they will flying during the night so they can sleep. They will have first class seats to have some room and will have a wheelchair and easy access to getting on the plane. Please pray for them as they make this long trip. This will be the first time Luke has been out of the hospital and rehab, so we hope he reacts well to the change and long trip. The doctors have said that his recovery will speed up when he gets home to familiar things, family, and friends. We will have to evaluate where he is at and where we will continue getting help. We are continuing to pray for full recovery.

In around a year, Luke will have to have surgery to put a plate in his head where the skull has been removed. They say this will again boost his recovery. Pray specifically for when that might take place and other details. We are praying that God would take care of it and surgery will not be necessary.

He is a great God and is still alive and working today! He has answered so many of our prayers and those of thousands who have walked with us. He isn't finished yet! We pray He will continue to be glorified through what has happened and that God will use Luke's testimony to help others. Pray that he will continue to regain his memory. Each day we see more and more of his memory coming together and everything making sense.

• • • • •

Thank You, Lord, for being here with me each step of the way. Your presence has sustained me. Thank You for giving me strength when I was so weary. Thank You for bringing help to me in my time of trouble to pray, encourage, and help in other ways. I thank You, Lord. Amen.

Kathy Bernard

Reflections

_____

_____

_____

_____

_____

_____

_____

_____

_____

41
WELCOME HOME (DAY 51)

You have turned my mourning into joyful dancing. You have taken away my clothes of mourning and clothed me with joy. —Psalm 30:11 (NLT)

Sunday was a day of rejoicing as we welcomed Luke home. We met them at the airport at 7 a.m. in the morning with big hugs and smiles. Daniel and Luke took a red eye direct flight so they could sleep on the way. Mission accomplished with no problems! Luke has been resting more comfortably now, and we are believing he will continue to recover. Pray as we look for places and people to help him in his rehab.

As I reflected on his homecoming, I was reminded of the story in the Bible of the son who came home. Oh the excitement I know that father felt as he saw his son coming home. And I know that his son, although he felt unworthy, was probably excited to finally return. Can you imagine how our heavenly Father feels when we come home to Him? Even when we don't feel we deserve His love, He lets us know that He loves us and forgives us. He deeply desires a relationship with us and wants to be part of our lives. As we have reflected about what we have gone through in the last six weeks, I know we wouldn't have been able to handle our valley if not for God's love, mercy, grace, and faithfulness. God is still alive and active and wants to be part of our lives.

As we enter into another phase of recovery, we ask that you continue to pray in agreement with us that Luke will be restored completely. We still have a road to travel in his recovery and further surgery to fix his skull. Pray for the necessary finances Luke will need for medical expenses since he didn't have insurance. Pray that we have wisdom as we deal with all his personal business that God will give us insight and help as needed. We are excited how God has worked, but look forward to how He will use this event for His glory.

• • • • •

Lord, today I rejoice. You have taken my mourning and turned it into joy. You are worthy to be praised. I worship You for who You are and what You have done in my life. Thank You for Your faithfulness and love. Your mercies are new every morning. Amen.

Reflections

_____

_____

_____

_____

_____

_____

_____

_____

HE WENT WALKING AND TALKING AND PRAISING GOD
(DAY 66)

Those who wait on the Lord shall renew their strength. They shall mount up with wings like eagles. They shall run and not be weary, they shall walk and not faint. — Isaiah 40:31 (NKJV)

In the story of the lame man that was healed, the scripture says that when he was healed, "He entered the temple with them, walking and leaping and praising God" (Acts 3:8 NASB). We are seeing the same thing take place in modern times with Luke. Last week he had his first outing to the National Day of Prayer. The six weeks from his accident to his recovery was shown with pictures, and then he walked forward and prayed a prayer of thanksgiving to God. He thanked those who prayed for him and ended by saying, "God healed me!"

Many attending who had been with us in this journey through reading this blog, rejoiced with tears and thanksgiving at what the Lord had done. I have heard so many say how much Luke's miracle story has encouraged them in their faith.

We have been praying and believing that God will use this

accident for His glory. Yes, *your prayers* are effective, and God is still alive, active, and definitely in the miracle business.

Since we have been home, Luke has become more relaxed in his familiar surroundings and with family. He continues to regain his memory. We work with him daily until we can get him into rehab. We go next week to the doctor to get the scripts for rehab. Pray we get a good evaluation and obtain the help Luke needs for his full recovery. Pray that we get a good doctor to evaluate his head and his future surgery in several months.

We have been blessed with help from a local world renowned massage therapist who is working toward getting Luke to have full use of his back and neck and is helping with any muscle damage. Luke has shown so much progress just in two appointments. We have also been offered music therapy, which will help Luke and encourage him in music. We so appreciate those who have reached out to help us in this rehab process.

• • • • •

Thank You, Lord, You continue to give me strength as I leave this valley. Thank You for helping me when I was weary and faint of heart. Thank You for what You have done in my life. I know You will give me strength to face my future. Help me to praise You. Amen.

Reflections

_____

_____

_____

_____

_____

_____

_____

_____

_____

_____

43

WAIT PATIENTLY ON THE LORD
AND SEE YOUR HEALING
(DAY 81)

I waited patiently for God to help me; then he listened and heard my cry. He lifted me out of the pit of despair, out from the blog and the mire, and set my feet on a hard, firm path, and steadied me as I walked along.

—Psalm 40:1-2 (TLB)

Patience is a hard quality to have. We are always trying to "get it done" as quickly as possible. But God doesn't work that way. Sometimes He works slowly, and we have to trust Him for the outcome.

Luke has continually been improving in his recovery. Through the Brain Injury Association, we were able to get him into speech therapy. He was tested this week, and she will make up a treatment plan for Luke to help where he has weakness in his memory. He goes to the gym daily to work out with supervision. Next week we visit a doctor who will look at him for surgery. He will need a plate put in the place where his skull is missing. Pray for the right doctor to do the procedure *and* the right timing. Luke's body needs to be ready for another surgery.

He goes to a muscular message therapist who is helping his neck and back and with his standing, walking, etc. He has helped Luke a lot already and will enable Luke to get to the place where he can go through the surgery. We are hoping that we could do it as early as July.

Luke keeps busy daily with activities. Before the accident he was interested in photography, so we are pulling out the camera so he can work on remembering that art. A local photographer is willing to work with him. Luke's attitude is great and he is very positive. He knows God healed him and is trusting God for the eventual outcome. Pray he would stay encouraged and be patient in the healing and the future that God has in store for him.

We thank each of you who continue to lift him up daily. God has been so good in restoring him physically, mentally, emotionally, and spiritually. We believe God has done a deep work and has *big* plans for Luke. We will keep you posted on when the surgery is, so keep praying.

• • • • •

Lord, help me to be patient. I so easily get impatient with my situation and want to move forward without You. Help me allow You to work and not push forward without You. Help me to trust You for the outcome. Amen.

Reflections

_____

_____

_____

_____

_____

_____

_____

_____

_____

_____

PEACE, PEACE, WONDERFUL PEACE (DAY 90)

And the peace of God, which surpasses all understanding, will guard your hearts and your minds in Christ Jesus. –Philippians 4:7 (ESV)

God's peace is quite an interesting thing to experience. In tragic or stressful situations, how can we remain calm? Having hope in who *He is* and what *He can do* builds that trust in our Father. Jesus said, "Peace I give you…" He has extended this gift that the world cannot understand. They marvel at it from a human mindset, but it goes deeper than that because we are spiritually connecting with our Father. Through this life changing event, we have been able to experience God's peace at such a deep level and are so thankful that we have our Father to turn to in our time of need.

We are again praising God for more good news. Luke will be having his surgery to repair his head this coming Friday, June 21st. We went to the doctor this week to see his progress and when the surgery could happen. We were surprised when he said, "It looks good! When do you want to do the surgery?" Since Luke did not have insurance, we had to do research on how to get him covered. Government help through disability takes *too long*. Not only did God bring us insurance, but the same doctors that do that type of surgery in our area take Luke's insurance. Within two weeks we had insurance, an appointment with doctor, and scheduled surgery. Wow!

Luke is going twice a week to a speech therapist to help with his memory. We were happy with his test results. With the brain injury test, you can be mild, moderate, or severe in your memory loss. Luke tested *mild*. He will continue his sessions throughout the summer, working on areas of his memory that are weak. He is remembering more and more. His six months in LA are still a gray area with not much memory. He doesn't remember the accident at all. *But*, he does know who saved and healed him—*God!* We are excited to see how God is going to use this event to bring others to Him. Pray for the surgery and that it will be a quick recovery. Pray that his memory will be restored and for patience on Luke's part in the healing process. And lastly, pray for Luke that God will show him exactly where and what He wants for Luke's life.

• • • • •

Thank You, Lord, that I have this supernatural peace as I go through this valley. I know that You are with me and I don't have to be afraid. Thank You for holding me up and carrying me when I couldn't go on. Amen.

Kathy Bernard

Reflections

_____

_____

_____

_____

_____

_____

_____

_____

EPILOGUE

So much has happened since our journey through this crisis. Luke did get his skull replaced in June 2013, three months after the accident, whereas the doctors had originally said it would take a year for him to be ready for it. Another miracle of God's goodness and grace. Luke's insurance didn't work out because they didn't cover pre-existing conditions. I struggled with how Luke would ever pay for any of his medical bills, both in LA and his head surgery. We applied for help for all the bills in California, and God provided miraculously by covering all medical and rehab bills.

Locally, I talked to the hospital, and a woman suggested that I apply for help from the hospital. She said that they look at cases, and sometimes will cover the hospital bill. I applied and started praying. I still remember the day I got the phone call. I was standing in the kitchen and they said, "We are calling to let you know that the hospital bill has been taken care of." Luke only had to pay for the services of the doctor who gave him his new skull.

Several years after the accident, Luke requested his medical records so we could read through them. After reading them, we realized that his medical state was far worse than what we had thought. Luke should have died or been a vegetable for the rest of his life. There is no question that his recovery *was a miracle*. Even the doctor over the hospital in LA shared that it was a miraculous recovery. We serve a miracle working God.

Our prayers that this experience would be used to bring glory to God was answered in a way only God could orchestrate. About six months after Luke's accident, he was struggling with sleeping at night, a symptom that many brain injury patient's experience. But one night he fell into a deep sleep and had a vivid dream. The next morning he was excited. When he shared the details with us, we told him to write it down. We thought it would be good for his recovery process. Luke wrote ninety pages, which became a script called *The Favorite*. (Go to www.thefavoritemovie.com to see a short video done by CBN.)

The Favorite is based on the real experiences of Luke and his physical and spiritual transformation. The story is told through the life of two brothers. It is about a distanced and agitated son, hurt by what he perceived as favoritism for his brother, who vents his anger through professional fighting. *The Favorite* book was published in 2015 with the movie being released in 2018. We are praying and believing that this story and its message will touch thousands.

The End of the Journey

As I finish sharing my journey with you, I understand that not all journeys end like ours did. To those who did not get that miraculous recovery or the answer you wanted in your journey, I can only say, "I don't know 'the why,' but I know that God can be trusted." Someday our questions will be answered by Him. Someday we will see clearly *all* things, and have the answers to *all* our whys. He will give you everything you need to press on even when life is different and will never be the same again. You will have to choose every day to be thankful, praise Him, and rejoice. It is a choice that you make. I'm reminded of Psalm 100:4-5:

Enter his gates with thanksgiving and his courts with praise; give thanks to him and praise his name. For the Lord is good and his love endures forever.

Remember that after you come out of a valley, there is a mountain before you. I encourage you not to settle and live in the valley. Don't let defeat and depression be your friends. God has something for you outside your valley. He wants to use your pain and failures to bring glory to Him. There are those still in their valley of pain and hurt that need your encouragement and prayers. Start with meeting the needs of those still in their valley, and God will show you His plan for your life. I pray that God will use your valley to make you stronger and more reliant on Him. It doesn't matter how much Satan has stolen or destroyed in your life, God wants to give you abundant life. I leave you with our theme scripture that we held onto throughout our journey:

The thief comes to steal, kill and destroy; but I have come so that you may have life, and may have it abundantly.
                                        —John 10:10 (NASB)

Luke Bernard, who played Benjamin in The Favorite, was in a near fatal accident March 9, 2013.

Luke before the accident

First responders didn't think Luke would recover from the accident.

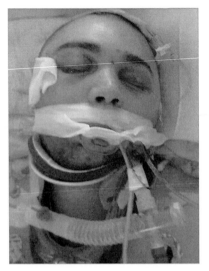

Luke arrived at L.A. County Hospital with a Glasgow Coma Scale of three with dilated and fixed pupils, given no hope for survival.

A piece of Luke's skull was removed to take out two blood clots and allow the damaged brain to swell, which helped keep him alive.

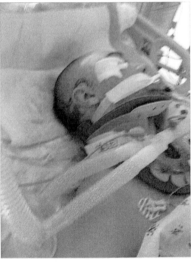

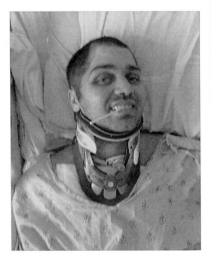

Luke miraculously woke up in eleven days and began a speedy recovery.

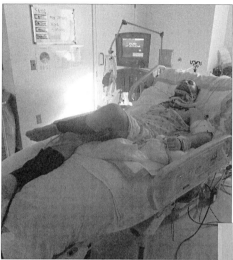

After seeing Luke move so much, Luke's parents requested more x-rays.

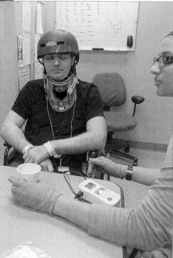

Luke had to learn how to swallow and eat solid foods again.

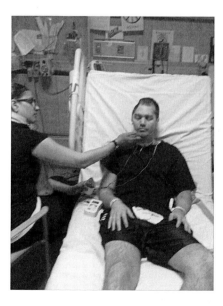

Luke in the midst of rehab.

Luke finished his rehabilitation in just three weeks!

Luke had to learn to do everything again, even writing his name.

After being home for two months, Luke shaved his head for his cranialplasty, new skull surgery. Joshua McKay, brother-in-law, and Luke's brother Peter, shaved their heads in support of his surgery.

Before surgery

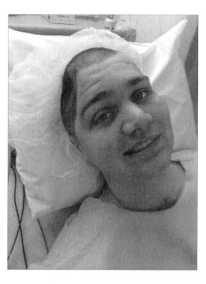

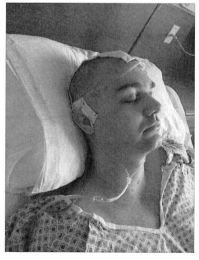

Luke's new skull after surgery

Daniel, Kathy, and Luke Bernard share their traumatic experience of God's miraculous work to encourage others through the book and movie, The Favorite.

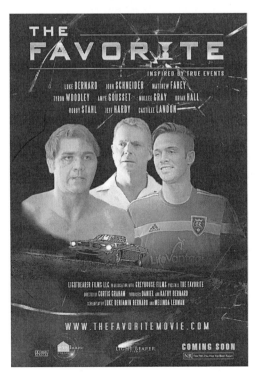

The movie poster for The Favorite.

About the Author

Kathy Bernard attended Johnson University (Florida campus), earning her B.S. degree She earned her Master's degree in Christian Education and Counseling at Cincinnati University where she met her husband, Daniel. They have been married for thirty-five years and have six children: Leah, Luke, Bethany, Faith, Peter, and Rachel. She enjoys being a Grandma to Ava and to Micah, who is arriving February 2018.

Kathy has ministered in a variety of arenas with her husband. They pastored churches in Williamstown, KY, and in Bryan, TX where Full House Ministries, Inc. was established. Through this ministry, they participated in outreach, such as street ministry and short-term mission trips, to Nigeria and Mexico. In January 1991, the Bernards began mission work in Nigeria, West Africa, planting churches and developing a discipleship school. Although the Bernards left the mission field in 1996, the work continues with nine established churches.

The Bernards then felt that God was leading them to Tampa Bay to work with the local churches. In December 1996, Somebody Cares, Tampa Bay was established to unify and empower the Church across denominational and racial lines, utilizing all the key components that are needed to effectively reach and evangelize the Bay area for Christ. Somebody Cares has equipped and supplied the Church with resources through many projects and events. By combining resources, they have been able to do more together than apart and significantly increase effectiveness in reaching the Bay area. For over twenty years, Kathy has actively administrated this work.

Kathy has also helped to edit the books Daniel writes. They co-authored a book on marriage, *Me Tarzan, You Jane!* (Evergreen Press). Kathy has been heavily involved in editing the book, *The Favorite*, as well as writing a prayer journal and study guide for *The Favorite* movie, coming to theaters in 2018.

The website for the movie
The Favorite
can be found at
www.thefavoritemovie.com
where you can also buy
Journey Through the Valley.
It is also available at Amazon and
Barnes & Noble January 2018